Copyright©2023 Julie E Craven

J C Publication

All Rights Reserved

ISBN 9781838495244

With Thanks

Ed Christiano, Director of Deeper Blue Marketing and Design Ltd
For cover template arrangement

Jason Packer
For proof reading

Daniel Craven
Computer advice and technical help

CONTENTS

1. My Fucking Knicker Elastic
3. Fuck Me You Naughty Duck
5. Bad Alphabet
7. Shut the Fucking Bird Up
9. Fuck Me, Poor Humpty Dumpty
11. Sex Mad Gnome
13. That Fucking Trout!
15. Santa's a Dirty Bastard!
17. I am a Little Thong
19. I Have a Beautiful Pussy
20. You Sad Bastard
23. Doggin'
25. Poor Fucking Toilet
27. Those Dick Head Visitors
29. It's Shitty Christmas Again
30. Oh Brother
31. Fucking Waste
33. Fucking Dog Shit
35. Bastard Fucking Seagulls!
36. Poor Friggin' Leprechaun
37. Mum Thinks I Look Like a Slapper
38. Oh Fuck, The Little Bastards
39. Those Fucking Threadworms
41. My Husbands Bollocks
42. I Hate to Clean One's Biz
43. My Humongous Fat Arse
44. Fucking Drunk Again
47. For Fucks Sake, My Glasses

48. Caterpillar's a Greedy Tosser
51. I am a Hampered Teacher
52. The Nudist Camp
55. Oh Shit, Work
56. I am a Fucking Perv
59. Oh Fuck, I am a Cleaning Sponge
60. Dam! My Fucking Hat
63. Bastard Spitting
64. I Love to Fart
67. Little Fucking Twat
69. Fuck me! A Flea
71. Our Neighbour's Flying Low
73. I Hate Bastard Worms
75. Big Fat Fucking Cow
77. I'm a Bumble Bee with a Big Prick
79. I Hate Fucking Wasps
81. FINALE

INTRODUCTION

I thought I'd write an adult book
Of poems to enjoy,
With lots of naughty little bits
Strategically deployed.

There're lots of many dirty words
Disgusting, filthy things,
All set-in place to add some umph,
Just read to see what brings.

They're not for people who will mind
Offended they may be,
As swear words there are many in,
This poem book, you'll see.

So please don't read this filthy book,
If you will take offense,
They're rude, blue, explicit and crude
And sometimes are intense!

MY FUCKING KNICKER ELASTIC

Oh fuck, it's the wrinklies outing,
We take them twice a year,
The seaside they all love to go,
They're filled with friggin' cheer.

The day is warm, with tiny breeze,
We've summer attire on,
Oh bastard twat, my knicker's slipped,
The elastic, it has gone!

I bent down quick to pick them up,
The breeze then lift my dress,
With arse on show and beaver creek,
What followed one can guess.

Poor Mable, she let out a shriek,
In shock she had to sit,
But Bob excited, eyes transfixed,
Upon my pussy bits.

Then Mable turned, gave Bob a slap,
He was a naughty boy,
When suddenly he burst his fly,
Out popped his little toy.

Poor Bob he grabbed his little prick,
As memories flooded back,
He'll have to wait to have a pull,
Sex drive he did not lack.

For Bob, his little light still shines,
He loved my down below,
The look and twinkle on Bob's face,
Would have loved a final blow.

I wish I could forget this day,
Unfortunately not,
But Mable had a treat in store,
Bob's cock, she got the lot!

FUCK ME YOU NAUGHTY DUCK

It's bath time now and friggin' fun.
As I'm dropped into the tub,
The water's on, the bubbles grow,
And sponge waits for the scrub.

I am a fucking little toy,
A duck is what I am,
And what delights I have to come,
When in steps my madam.

I look upon her great big tits,
And willy starts to rise,
If she sits down, madam will get,
A fucking huge surprise.

While sponge washed over her bulging breasts,
I pulled my willy quick,
As I tossed off and then let fly,
Her tits, it did the trick.

For now I'm sad, as madam's gone,
Cos bath times fucking fun,
I am a naughty little duck,
A wank, it must be done.

BAD ALPHABET

A is for arsehole, B is for ball sack
C is cunnilingus, when lay on one's back.

D is for dickhead, E is erotic,
F is for face fuck, described as euphoric.

G is for g-spot, H is for humping,
I for insertion, as one begins pumping.

J is for johnny bag, K for Karma Sutra,
L is for licking, I'm ready for shooting.

M is masturbation, N is for nipple,
O is for oral, swallow, spit or withdrawal.

P is penetration, Q is for quim,
R is for rimming, but this rather grim.

S is for sex, T is for tonguing,
U is urethra, which is part of one's plumbing.

V is vagina, W for wanking,
X is X-rated, might end in a spanking.

As I come to a close, with the alphabet batch,
Y can be yeast, which you'll find up one's Zatch.

SHUT THE FUCKING BIRD UP

I'm woke up in the morning,
Oh twat as the blackbird sings,
But fuck, I'd rather have my sleep,
Than the friggin' noise it brings!

It sits upon the bastard branch,
I'd love to knock it down,
"Go and pester some other fuck,
Piss off you fucking clown."

It isn't time to get up yet,
I need to fucking sleep,
So all you singing bastard birds,
Fuck off before I weep.

Thank Christ the little twat has gone,
It's peace I have at last,
But when night falls, he sings again,
Oh shit and fucking blast!

FUCK ME, POOR HUMPTY DUMPTY

There is an egg which is spoken in rhyme,
Fuck me, it's Humpty Dumpty.
He came about from mother hen,
From fucking rumpy pumpy.

How Humpty Dumpty came about,
Up on this bastard wall,
It baffled me, as to how he did,
As he wasn't friggin' tall.

Was those Queens horses and arsehole men,
The horrible nasty twats,
Which went and put poor Humpty Dumpty,
Up on the wall like that.

Fucking bollocks, they all had a plan,
Was all about Humpty's demise,
A Royal conspiracy, one could say,
Poor Humpty, they said he's to die!

The bloody bastards, the next thing you knew,
What wankers! Poor Humpty was pushed,
Those Queens men did it, the heartless twats,
For it had to be all fucking hushed.

Humpty cracked open, out popped his brain,
To mend him, oh fuck, they tried,
Was from this day on, that Humpty made fame,
Remembered in death cos he died.

SEX MAD GNOME

I am a horny little gnome,
And love my willie dearly,
I wank beside a lily pond,
Where frogs all watch right near me.

I have a big tit girlfriend gnome,
Which I sometimes get to shag,
She often plays with my big cock,
But I'm not one to brag.

I love to do it doggy style,
So I can slap her arse,
And hold her tits and squeeze them tight,
As I say I am her marse.

Today must be my lucky day,
A fuck is what I wished for,
My girlfriend gnome shows me her tits,
As I shag her and much more.

THAT FUCKING TROUT

I'm sitting by the riverside,
Fishing in the still,
I've rod in hand and net by side,
As river flows downhill.

My line pulls tight, but what is this?
A great big fucking trout!
It tugs and pulls with all it's might,
In fear I think, no doubt.

I lose my balance and fall in,
The water's friggin' freezing!
My cock and balls have shrivelled up,
Which is awfully displeasing.

This bastard trout, I wheel it in,
While cock and balls turn blue,
I place this fucking trout ground,
Then whacked it with my shoe.

It now laid dead, thank fuck for that,
Destined for my plate,
Beheaded, gutted, grilled, and skinned,
Oh fuck, I was irate.

A fitting end for this bastard trout,
As my cock and balls thawed out,
All nice and warm in my wives' hands,
Oh dear, I've grown a spout!

SANTA'S A DIRTY BASTARD

There was one year, Santa I caught,
Upon my blessed roof,
The dirty bastard was wanking his knob,
For this is the friggin' truth!

He stood up there with knob in hand,
Giving it a great big pull,
He leaned right over my chimney pot,
Cock and balls as big as bull.

It silhouetted in moon light,
And looked like steel erecting,
He pulled and fucking pulled some more,
Ready for ejaculating.

Oh fucking bollocks, what a shock,
To see him masturbating,
Fuck me, he's gone and shot his load,
Which landed on my grating.

This sheds a different fucking light,
For this I now do fear,
Cos Santa came right down my chimney,
As he comes just once a year.

I AM A LITTLE THONG

My home is in a bedroom drawer,
Until I'm taken out,
Then placed upon a curly minge,
It's what it's all about.

But part of me is pulled into,
A great big smelly crack,
Which covers up one's big arsehole,
What hygiene she does lack!

Sometimes I see a tiny string,
Oh fuck, the commies are here,
As long as it's kept controlled inside,
A flood I need not fear.

The filthy cow, what does she eat?
Her farts they smell so foul!
Bugger me, the thought of the shit,
Which lies inside her bowel.

But when it comes to coughs and sneezes,
She leaks a drop of piss,
It's not this wet I love and long,
Her juice I really miss.

I am a tiny little thong,
A minge I'm placed upon,
If hairy minge is well concealed,
My job has then been done.

I HAVE A BEAUTIFUL PUSSY

Has one ever thought about the pussy,
How beautiful one is.
They come in many a different shape,
And loved, they are the biz.

The pussy always loves a stroke,
When given half a chance,
This lovely, wanting, hairy thing,
All ready for the pounce.

Some are hairless, always bald,
And smooth with all to see.
We notice all the nooks and crannies,
But this is meant to be.

When pussy's splayed out on the bed,
And laid with legs apart,
But looks relaxed and so contented,
Then fuck, lets out a fart.

Oh fucking hell, we got crossed wires,
This is my pussy cat,
I'm talking of my beautiful pet,
And not some little twat!

YOU SAD BASTARD

The sun is shining brightly,
With a tiny little breeze,
So fuck, I'll put my mini on,
And flash my pretty knees.

I fucking love this number,
As I know it's friggin' cute,
Because sad bastard men in cars,
Will give a little toot.

So I fucked off to wonder,
To show off my great legs,
And it wasn't long before,
Sad bastards turned their heads.

Fuck me, a man then whistled,
His horn he then did press,
When shit, along came wind,
And lifted up my dress.

The car then hit a lamppost,
As I fucking looked in ponder,
Had sad bastard never seen,
Some knickers I did wonder.

I then rushed, and pissed off quick,
As home I had to run,
And found out to my amazement,
Fuck me, I'd got none on!!!

DOGGIN'

I thought I'd have a day trip out,
Up in the countryside.
And parked the car in country lane,
Not many, far and wide.

There were a few cars parked nearby,
All close, next to each other,
But when I looked, fuck me, my God,
Tit wank, knob end, oh brother.

I couldn't help but stop and watch,
Frig me, it was exciting,
One man was cunnilingus deep,
His cock was so inviting.

A woman's lips locked onto this,
Oh fuck, it was a mouthful,
Was like an orgy in a film,
Some might have said it sinful.

I went and spied the next in line,
A man there was balls deep,
With woman there astride on top,
Both in a fucking heap.

I moved along to see some more,
Was last car in the line,
Now faced with fat arse in the air,
Performing the sixty-nine.

I now was feeling rather moist,
And joined in rather quick,
A man said, "Get your laughing gear,
Around my great big prick."

Oh what a fun filled shagging day,
This doggin' lark is great,
With lots of knob end, fuck faced sucks,
It must have all been fate.

POOR FUCKING TOILET

If only toilets had a voice,
What shitty tales they'd tell,
Of all which sits upon the bog,
And dangle down the well.
      There're those which sit to have a shit,
      Who push but only gas,
      Comes forth with gust, the fucking smell,
      Straight from one's big fat arse
It isn't friggin' funny, when those who've been,
To dine and eaten curry,
For fuck me, the very next day,
The bog, as they must hurry.
      They sit upon the bog with haste,
      Not long before shit comes,
      The crap which pebble dashes round,
      The basin, fuck it hums!
When constipation troubles come,
A lot to comprehend,
Why one's shit when pushed on through,
Will fucking block the bend.
      When cheeks a spread and one must guess,
      What bastard parcels come,
      From soft to hard and rabbit bobs,
      Oh fuck, we want to run.
We sigh with glee when only pee,
Is pissed around the pot,
Until next time, we'll have to see,
Might get the shitting lot!!!

THOSE DICK HEAD VISITORS

Oh bloody hell, who's at the door,
I'll have to go down and see.
Through frosted glass, two figures I spy,
Oh shit, don't let it be.

Those annoying twats who come in pairs,
If only people knew.
No guesses who, you've probably had,
On your doorstep seen a few.

One tries to say firmly, fuck off, not now,
Go pester some other poor fuck.
But why do these bastards, keep persisting,
And gamble on pushing their luck.

It's a pity the cunts have no job to do,
But bore us with all their shit!
Oh bloody fuck, they're still at the door,
As they knock and never quit.

Oh thank the Lord, it's started to rain,
Maybe God is taking a piss.
As pissing down, in buckets it is,
They're gone, now it's fucking bliss!!!

IT'S SHITTY CHRISTMAS AGAIN

It's shitty Christmas now again,
Oh fuck, it costs a lot!
The little bastard's lists are long,
I think they've lost the plot!

A fucking bank I'll have to rob,
The price of just one game.
Oh crap, if that's not bad enough,
A console one could name.

What friggin' robbing twats they are,
A game's a piece of plastic,
They have us by the short and curli's
The twats, it is so drastic!

The crappy tree is up again,
Thank God that this is done,
Putting the balls up one by one,
It isn't fucking fun!

We've mistletoe and friggin' holly,
With lights put on at night,
For now it's done, thank fuck for that,
This Christmas lark is shite!!!

OH BROTHER

My brother had two budgerigars,
Fuck me, called Mork and Mindy,
We pissed our sides at their two names,
But could have been Dick and Mingy.

He bought them fucking lots of toys,
To play with, oh what joy,
The twats would play, make lots of noise,
Mistake it was, oh boy.

"Shut the fuck up, you noisy twats,
Before I wring your neck,"
He tried in vain to stop the chirps,
But they would only peck.

A selfish twat my brother was,
He gave them both away
Where they now chirp with my dear mother,
Thank fuck, they now can play.

FUCKING WASTE

Fuck me, its bloody bin men day,
As the fucking cart draws near,
To empty all our shit and crap,
Which stinks in the atmosphere.

A peg I need upon my nose,
As I whiff this bastard smell,
It's all the waste scraped off one's plate,
It stinks like fucking hell.

But what has made this fishy smell,
Oh fuck, could be the wife,
It may be all her piss flap rags,
Which makes it jam rag rife.

My waste in bin, toxic it is,
Thank God it's got a lid,
The fumes concealed, thank fuck for that,
As away in cart it's slid.

FUCKING DOG SHIT

It's the same fucking story,
I've said it before,
Watch out for the dog shit,
That's left on the floor.

It's the poor friggin' kids,
All happy at play,
While dick head dog owners,
Leave dog shit all day!

The kids play some football,
As kids love to do,
Oh fuck, in the distance,
A huge lump of poo!

The bastard and dick head,
Who left the shit there,
All smelly, disgusting,
And don't fucking care!

Irresponsible twats,
Who all should be fined,
Cos their dogs only shit,
On what they have dined!

I picked up this lump,
It was her dog next door,
Her letter box it went,
On her fucking floor!

Well, when all's said and done,
If you love your hound,
Don't just be a bastard twat!
Pick up your fucking mound!!!

BASTARD FUCKING SEAGULLS

I live at the seaside for my bastard sins,
Where people throw rubbish, but not in the bins.
And walk down the coastline as I'm filled with woes,
Fucking rubbish and bird shit where everyone goes!

Then along come the seagulls, my peace is then
Shattered,
They fly overhead, oh fuck, I've been splattered!
The dirty bastards, it dripped down my face,
I've splats on my T-shirt, I'm in the wrong place!

It smelt fucking putrid, I wanted to puke,
I'd get rid of the bastards, if only could nuke.
I searched in my pocket, thank God that I found,
A clean piece of snot rag, to wipe off the mound.

I knew these big bastards were laughing at me,
A chance which you take when you live at the sea.
It's said and it's true, they're a shit machine,
Bird shit at the seaside, forever we clean!

POOR FRIGGIN' LEPRECHAUN

I'm a poor friggin' leprechaun,
For all my bastard sins,
And have to live inside a boot,
With my arsehole siblings!

The boot is small and tightly packed,
We all sleep top-to-toe,
But when one farts, fuck me, the smell,
It stifles one's airflow!

Oh shit, the snoring I endure,
I lose my bastard sleep!
A slap or two will frigging do,
There's not another peep.

Our neighbours are nosey tossers,
When we have to take a shit,
For the garden is our God sent loo,
Where we do our shitting bit.

I'm a poor friggin' leprechaun,
I suffer one's farts and snores,
It's with my arsehole siblings,
And I have to shit outdoors!!!

MUM THINKS I LOOK LIKE A SLAPPER

Mum thinks I look like a slapper,
Fuck that, as I go out.
My shorts are tight and arse looks great,
Bang tidy one could shout.

Mum thinks I look like a slapper,
My arse cheeks are on show,
But arse is firm, looks fucking great,
Not like a lump of dough.

Mum thinks I look like a slapper,
Cos my tits are bulging out,
Nipples erect, cleavage on show,
A good tit wank, no doubt!

Mum thinks I look like a slapper,
Both tits and arse on show,
With arse bang tidy, tits for wanky,
The modern girl, you know.

I'm not a fucking slapper,
For this is what we wear,
At least my twat is not on show,
Wouldn't want to cause despair!!!

OH FUCK, THE LITTLE BASTARDS!

I set off in my motor car,
When driving down the road,
Some bastard kids step out on me,
No fucking 'Green Cross Code'!

The little twats, my brakes slam on,
As they just looked and grinned,
"You fucking dick heads," I shouted out,
But they were all thick skinned!

It's now a fact these modern times,
Jay walk they fucking do!
The bleeding cunts just stroll across,
WHEN IT SHOULD BE TABOO!

There are so many pricks about,
Which need a friggin' crack!
I'd love to see the smile knocked off,
And give their face a smack!

These little bastards will one day,
Be big bastards no doubt!
And then whilst driving in their cars,
Some arsehole kids step out!!!

THOSE FUCKING THREADWORMS!

Threadworms, threadworms, threadworms galore,
My arsehole is a tickling, I think I'm getting more.
They start to wiggle all about as I squeeze my arsehole tight,
The bastards like to lay their eggs whilst I'm fast asleep at night.

They slip outside my arsehole, to get their duty done,
But they fucking won't stop tickling, so I go to scratch my bum!
Eggs get up my friggin' nails, without me even knowing,
And because they're microscopic, there's nothing which is showing.

So when getting out of bed, and downstairs I then do trot,
I never washed my fucking hands, as I just clean forgot!
I went and ate my breakfast, and then passed onto my toast,
Those twatting eggs from up my nails, under my unsuspecting nose!

So now all my breakfast's eaten, and everything digested,
I have to now inform you, I've been fucking re-infested!
Now, if ever you get threadworms, a chemist you must see,
And make sure you wash and scrub your nails, so you'll be threadworm free!!!

MY HUSBANDS BOLLOCK'S

I cup my husband's bollocks,
As this it is a must,
Feeling each bollock with my hand,
Examine them! not lust!

You dirty bastard, it's not for sex,
I'm feeling them for lumps!
Manipulating both his balls,
Relieved when there's no bumps!

As cancer is the major fact,
The bollocks must be checked,
That your crown jewels are lumpy free,
It's easy to inspect!

It only takes a minute to,
Inspect for peace of mind,
So grab your bollocks by the hand,
And hope that you don't find.

Or maybe you could ask the wife,
If not, go find a trollop,
So when undressed, do take the test,
And check your fucking bollocks!!!

I HATE TO CLEAN ONE'S BIZ!

I am a hampered toilet roll,
Wipe arses all day long,
Apprehension best describes my thoughts,
When I have to face the pong!

I wipe piss flaps to clean one's pee,
And love to clean those twats,
But my main job's to deal with shit,
Those great big filthy cracks!

The type of shit from one's rear end,
Disgusting really is,
As I'm squashed into one's smelly crack,
To clean away the biz!

Ring pieces come in many forms,
From tight, right through to baggy,
The tight hole is a one-way street,
Where baggie's had lots of shaggy!

There's not a lot which I can do,
A shit wipe isn't fun,
As I'm dropped and sink below biz mark,
My job has now been done!

MY HUMONGOUS FAT ARSE

I stuffed my face this Christmas,
My arse is bulging out,
The waist is like a fucking tyre,
A dress size up, no doubt!

My bastard waist is squishy,
As I feel my shitty flab,
I'm shocked as in the mirror see,
Great handfuls I can grab!

For fucks sake, what a bastard mess!
My friggin' arse no peach!
There're no back scuttles now for me,
His fucking cock won't reach!

I've pot holes on my humongous arse,
My navel's disappeared,
Tummies covered my little twat,
A front bum has appeared!

No rumpy pumpy now for me,
Cos I'm a fucking mess!
My cunt is lost amongst the fat!
As I burst out from my dress!!!

FUCKING DRUNK AGAIN!

A friend of mine he had some drinks,
Too fucking many I'd say,
As he got up to head for home,
And tried to make his way.

He staggered through the friggin' door,
And stepped onto the path,
To watch was like a comedy sketch,
Waiting for the aftermath.

The twat he staggered up the street,
But fell under a bush,
Fuck me, there was no head to see,
Me trying to keep him hush.

The silly cunt, I pulled him up,
Without us being seen,
And tried to get him home intact,
From where he had just been.

I got the toss pot through his gate,
Where he fell a second time,
This time it was between plant pots,
Straight in a fucking line.

All one could see was two big feet,
Which peeped around the pot,
The rest of him was covered with,
Not one pot but the lot!

Fuck me I tried to pick him up,
This time without success,
He'd now disturbed his moron wife,
Who came to see his mess.

I tried again to pull him up,
But farted with the strain,
His wife had only fucking thought,
He'd shit himself again!

At last we got him through the door,
And up the stairs to sleep,
Thank fuck for that, ordeal's now done,
With not a friggin' peep!!!

FOR FUCKS SAKE, MY GLASSES

I'm supposed to wear my glasses,
Upon my bastard nose,
To help me see what lies in front,
Cos it's how it fucking goes.

Fuck me, I forgot to put them on,
I am a stupid prick,
Could say I am a toss pot,
As thick as a fucking brick!

Oh fuck, my phone gives out a ping,
Which dick head's text me now?
For I can't see a twatting thing,
To read It, don't know how.

I try to squint, no fucking good,
The tosser will have to wait,
But it only goes and pings some more,
"Fuck off," I'm in a state!

It's my responsibility,
I am a stupid twat!
No glasses on my bastard nose,
No fucking fun in that!!!

CATERPILLAR'S A GREEDY TOSSER

I have a greedy caterpillar,
She eats all fucking day,
The more she eats, the more she shits,
Which adds to my dismay.

She's in a pissing jam jar,
I watch the little twat,
Who tries to hide behind a leaf,
Fuck me, again she's shat!

But when I woke one morning,
The tossing twat had gone,
I looked around the bastard jar,
It wasn't fucking on!

Well fuck it, as the jar I put,
Onto my windowsill,
I left it there for quite some time,
All quiet and in the still.

But when at last I got this jar,
Oh fucking bollocks, what's this?
I now do have a butterfly,
Oh shit, what did I miss!

From caterpillar to cabbage white,
She's now a butterfly,
When out of jar, is where she then,
Fucked off into the sky.

I AM A HAMPERED TEACHER

Another bastard day at school,
I am a hampered teacher,
And hate the horrid snotty kids,
Which is my daily feature.

They're so unruly on their phones,
And act like stupid dick heads!
They fuck about, act the fool,
It's what a teacher dreads!

We're not allowed to fucking touch,
Or take away their phone,
If only they could understand,
But all they do is moan!

They need their English and their maths,
As education matters!
If they fuck up, the stupid twats,
Their life will end in tatters!

The moral is as plain to see,
Don't be a stupid dick head,
Put down your phone, don't be a twat,
And strive to be well read!!!

THE NUDIST CAMP

How funny is the nudist camp,
With all those different pricks.
Knob ends galore to feast upon,
A choice of hand-held sticks.

Fuck me, a man he went to bend,
With arse stuck in the air,
The bollocks dangling there between,
A bull you could compare.

Just look at all the ladies' tits,
With many a different size.
The older ladies' tits gone south,
Would never win a prize.

They flop and sway and fucking bounce,
Which makes one's cock atingle,
One has to slap it down real quick,
To allow a chance to mingle.

One watches all the minges bare,
They even have a haircut,
But some are bald, oh fuck, what's this?
Twats like a camel's foot.

Just think of their bare bums on seat,
All spread where they all sit,
OH FUCK, a man has just stood up,
And left a smear of shit!

Not just the arse one has to watch,
It's also women's fannies,
Which leaves a wet spot from their slit,
But nothing from old grannies.

But when one farts when sat on seat,
OH FUCK, it is so funny!
But mind you, if followed through,
Fuck faced if it's all runny!

It's funny in a nudist camp,
Could be a knocking shop,
But what if all is past their prime,
Would make ones' willy flop.

If a shag is what you're after,
And want to dip your dingler,
Don't book into a nudist camp,
Go find some fucking swinger!

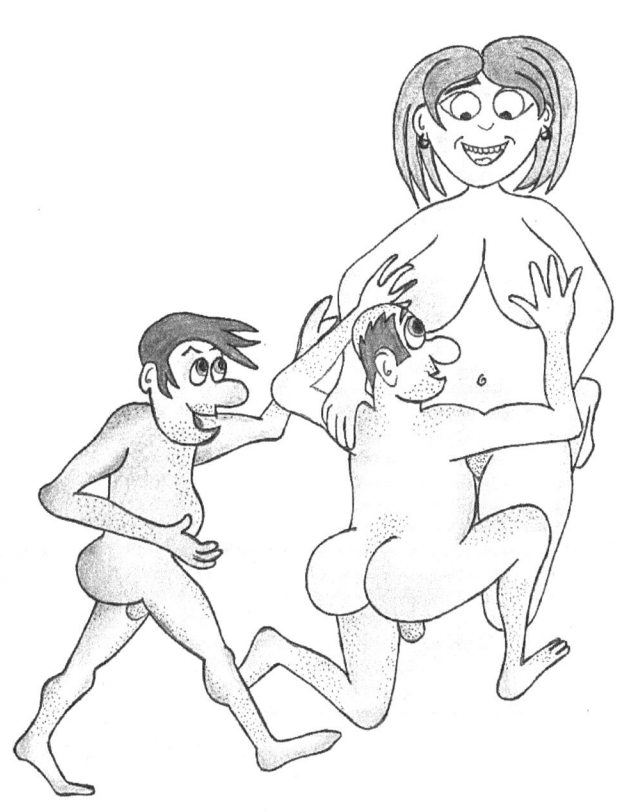

OH SHIT, WORK

Oh fuck, it's four in the morning,
I start at frigging six.
The early shift, I am a twat,
As I join the other pricks.

At least I'm not a lazy fuck!
No benefits for me!
I'm not a shitty, dick head dosser,
And don't get things for free.

My job involves good exercise,
I'll not get big and fat,
I move a lot and never stop,
I'm no bone idol twat!

Thank God I'm paid to exercise,
As I hate the fucking gym!!!
I'm a fit fuck, bang tidy bitch,
But deffo, never prim!!!

I AM A FUCKING PERV!

I fucking love the coffee shops,
And watch the world pass by,
With lots of naked skin to see,
So many a naked thigh.

Some thighs are bigger than my waist,
Up to the fannies top,
Imagination next to none,
Make many a man's flies pop.

Was not like this in bygone days,
Where all was covered up,
Oh bugger, how boring and what prudes,
OH BASTARD, SHIT, OH FUCK.

Not now, we watch the tits bounce by,
    Some bulging looking like jelly.
A good tit wank what comes to mind,
    Then plop upon ones' belly.

Sometimes a big fat arse walks past,
    With skirt right up to minge.
The thought of what lies there beneath,
    Maybe a curly fringe?

We're not so bothered what one wears,
    Go flash your perfect bits,
    If everybody's happy then,
    GO FUCK the prudish gits!

OH FUCK, I AM A CLEANING SPONGE!

OH FUCK, I am a cleaning sponge,
I scrub away the day,
A day what's packed with shitty tasks,
For I don't have a say.

I have to wash ones' cock and balls,
And lots of minges too,
But when it comes to wash the arse,
Sometimes I'm faced with poo!

I start to break out in a sweat,
And want to fucking cry!
As I'm squashed into a stinky crack,
To wash one's big arse eye.

I'm smeared with shit, it knocks me sick,
As I clean around this crevice,
Until the muck is washed away,
It's a fucking ball ache menace!!!

DAM! MY FUCKING HAT!

Whilst walking in the park one day,
The wind was fucking freezing!
I thought I'd better wear my hat,
Cos I can't stop friggin' sneezing.

Fuck me, my cock has shrivelled up,
My blood has all withdrawn.
But whilst concerned about my cock,
My fucking hat was gone!

My poor hat in the distance blew,
As I hurried on ahead,
The twatting hat now worse for wear,
To lose it I did dread!

Thank fuck, it stuck by litter bin,
Cos I'm out of fucking breath!
I coughed and wheezed but hurried up,
Before I caught my death.

A lady went to pick it up,
As I tried to hurry more,
"That's mine," I shouted, "You fuck off,"
So was thrown back on the floor.

She then pissed off and left my hat,
Right there just by the bin,
So I grabbed my dirty, dishevelled hat,
Then home for a bloody gin!

BASTARD SPITTING!

I don't know why it is today,
Bastards spit on the floor,
The dirty fucks, along their way,
Or any place they go!

I have to walk along and look,
The footpath there to see,
Oh shit, I've stood on grolly and,
It's fucking stuck on me!!

Oh knob and bastard, dirty twats!
The germs which there may be!
Tuberculosis, viruses,
It's all which we can't see!

So take heed, you stupid pricks,
Next time you get a bit,
Just swallow the little fucking thing,
And pass it in your shit!!!

I LOVE TO FART

Has one ever thought about the fart,
Which sneaks out from one's bum?
The different fucking noises made,
And the many farts which hum.

So amusing often it can be,
And equally embarrassing,
Depending on who's round about,
And who you're friggin' gassing.

Some farts do have a pungent smell,
Depending on what's eaten,
Hot and silent and most deadly,
The ones which can't be beaten.

Some people say that they've passed wind,
And some may say they've pumped,
Others may say they've had a fart,
The rest could say they've trumped.

There're farts which play a fucking tune,
Which last a good few seconds,
But some come forth with a mighty blast,
With another one that beckons.

The fart it is a funny thing,
With different sounds it gives us,
Depending on the size of bum,
And the tightness of one's annus.

A fat arse gives a muffled sound,
And tight arse gives a squeak,
A slack arse who knows what to come,
And what lies up their creek.

When farts let rip in nudist camp,
One hopes one is not near,
Just in case a wet one's brewed,
Which pebbles from one's rear.

Some people get disgusted,
To hear one's fart let rip,
But I blow off when needed,
As one's stomach would give the jip.

One could say it's a slight explosion,
From one's arse where gas breaks free,
When said and done it's normal,
So fuck off, what will be will be!

LITTLE FUCKING TWAT

There is a naughty fucking boy,
Who is a little twat!
You may think this way too harsh,
But he's called much more than that!

When daddy longlegs takes to flight,
This awful little shit,
Will pull their legs off one by one,
The bastard little prick!

Oh fuck, he has a catapult,
In comic he got free,
Watch out as stones go hurtling past,
At birds, he does with glee!

A magnifying glass he has,
The scrote, uses sun's rays,
He burns those poor, fucking bugs,
This dick head does for days!

Poor butterflies, the bastard gets,
A board he pins them to,
All different species if he can,
If only people knew!

Oh fuck, he has a chemistry set,
Experiments he does,
A fucking stink set off in school,
The knob! He gets a buzz!

I wish this fucking little twat,
When older, for all this loss,
Gets, burnt, gassed, and fucking pinned,
Upon a great big cross!!!

FUCK ME! A FLEA!

Fuck me, I can't stop itching,
I have to fucking scratch!
My bastard itch won't go away,
Hope it isn't one to catch.

Is it a flea within my clothes?
Oh fuck, knob end, tit wank!
If it's a flea that itches me,
The cat I'll have to thank!

It's from the bogging garden,
Hopped in cat's friggin' fur,
I've now got lumps, I'm bloody bit!
And all cat does is purr!

The flea it is elusive,
Impossible to track,
I'll get the fucking bastards,
Strong will I do not lack!

I got myself some flea spray,
Ripped off my pissing clothes,
And gassed the tosser vampires,
Now dead, I do suppose!

OUR NEIGHBOUR'S FLYING LOW

It often has been said and true,
Our neighbour goes commando,
He likes his wedding tackle loose,
With nothing tight below.

He wears no bastard underpants,
Cos he doesn't like restriction,
And lets the air blow round his balls,
So he doesn't suffer friction.

Oh fuck, one day he's flying low,
And doesn't realise,
He'd set off out and only had,
Forgot to zip his fly!

Now unaware of what he'd done,
Oh shit! Out popped his willy,
He'd only realised because,
It felt so friggin' chilly!

He popped his dick inside so quick,
Then looked around to see,
If anyone had seen his knob,
Whilst it had broken free.

When zipping up his bloody fly,
He trapped his fucking foreskin!
Which brought some tears into his eyes,
Where does he now begin?

He yanked it quick, OH GOD, my prick!
Nearly fainted on the spot!
His little prick now worse for wear,
Cos, to zip he had forgot!

I HATE BASTARD WORMS!

Whilst out in the garden digging one day,
Up popped a fucking worm.
Fuck me, wasn't funny as it made me jump!
When will I friggin' learn!

This worm didn't bother as it fucked on by,
But made me pissing fall!
The twat, my arse now full of mud!
To clean, I'd bugger all!

I picked the fucker up as it wiggled and squirmed,
Then over my neighbour's wall.
It landed in their pond as I heard a splash.
Then eaten, was the worm's downfall!!!

BIG, FAT, FUCKING COW

I am a big, fat, fucking cow,
In field I stand with others,
We piss and shit on farmer's land,
Until we fill our udders.

We have to friggin' stand and wait,
Our udders are now full!
Oh fuck, I think they're going to burst,
Already for the pull.

The shit-head farmers late again!
To take us to the shed,
And have our great big tits sucked dry.
For this we fucking dread!

We blame it on the bastard bull!
It's all his bollock's fault!
For what is shot from big bulls' cock,
Could call it an assault!

Then out pops calf, the milks-a-flow,
What damage cock has done!
We're now a fucking milk machine!
Cos big bollocks had his fun!!!

A BUMBLE BEE WITH A BIG PRICK!

I am a big fat bumble bee,
In flowers I nip in quick,
I fuck along with buzzing song,
Armed with a great big prick!

A prick that's placed upon my arse,
Which sits there standing proud,
A prick I hope which I can use,
To make one shout out loud.

I fucking love it when you cry,
It fills me with much glee,
I'm not just here to pollinate,
My prick I'll guarantee!

Fuck me, you run when I pass by,
But I friggin' don't care less,
As I love to stick my prick in quick,
Regardless of your stress.

I am this fucking bumble bee,
Armed with a great big prick,
I flit around with prick stood proud,
And stick it in real quick!!!

I HATE FUCKING WASPS!

A wasp has fucking stung me,
Right on my friggin' shitter!
Oh fuck it hurts that I could cry,
The bastard little critter!

I dropped my kecks to take a look,
Fuck me, my arse was red!
But couldn't pull the sting out when,
It filled me with much dread!

Someone will have to suck it out,
Good job I'm not alone,
"Come here and slap your lips on this,"
"Fuck off! And stop your groan."

"You selfish twat," I shouted out,
With fucking arse in pain,
"If shoe was on the other foot,
I'd help you just the same".

"No twatting chance that I will suck,
There on your shitty arse"!
What started off as serious,
Turned into a bloody farse!

I sadly pulled up bloody pants,
With arse now swollen out,
The bastard cunt, he wouldn't help,
I'll have to do without!

FINALE

I hope you liked my filthy poems,
And thought them all disgusting,
I loved to use those shocking words,
No need for re-adjusting.

They're rude, blue and fucking crude,
I hope they hit the spot,
Those awful words one hears a lot,
All added to the plot.

The cover warned of what lay in,
Adult material wrote,
So if you bought because of this,
One must love a dirty joke.

I'll end off now, my book is done,
Oh shit, knob end, tit wank,
Until next time, maybe, who knows,
If my mind is not a blank.

GOOD BYE

www.ingramcontent.com/pod-product-compliance
Lightning Source LLC
Chambersburg PA
CBHW041309110526
44590CB00028B/4298